Contents

Any words appearing in the text in bold, **like this**, are explained in the glossary.

Queen for an age

Queen Victoria was Britain's **monarch** for longer than any other. Because she reigned for so long (1837–1901), she gave her name to the Victorian age. Not just queen of Britain, she was also the head of the British **Empire**. There are statues and **monuments** to Victoria in countries she never saw.

A time of change

During Victoria's long life, she saw many changes. She was born into a world of horse-drawn carriages, but later travelled on steam trains and rode in motor cars. She lived through the **industrial revolution**, which made Britain the 'workshop of the world'.

Victoria was the first British queen to be photographed and filmed, the first to have her head pictured on stamps, the first to use a telephone, and the first to hear her own voice recorded by a machine.

In her own words

Her journeys were described in books and newspapers. She kept a diary for most of her life, and she was a tireless letter-writer to her government and to her children. So we know a lot about Victoria from her own words.

▲ There are statues of Victoria in many **Commonwealth** countries. This one is in Kensington Gardens, in London.

▲ **This Victorian map shows the British Empire at its peak, in about 1900. Victoria was queen of a quarter of the world, and almost a quarter of its people.**

The events and inventions of Victoria's remarkable age shaped the modern world. Although she lived quietly for much of her life, Victoria's name was known around the world because during her reign Britain was the most powerful country on earth.

Victoria did not make laws or lead **revolutions**, yet this tiny woman had such a mighty presence that when she died, many people felt that it was a turning point in history. They called it 'the Victorian Age'.

Key dates

1819	Victoria born in London
1837	Victoria becomes queen
1840	Victoria marries Prince Albert
1851	Opening of the Great Exhibition
1861	Prince Albert dies
1876	Victoria is named **Empress** of India
1887	Victoria's Golden Jubilee
1897	Victoria's Diamond Jubilee
1901	Queen Victoria dies

The little princess

Victoria was born into a royal family in trouble. Her father was the Duke of Kent, the fourth son of King George III. The king was old and mentally ill. His eldest son, the Prince **Regent**, acted as king. The Prince Regent was very vain and the **monarchy** was unpopular.

Victoria's parents

The Duke of Kent, a soldier, had married in 1818 at the age of 50. His wife was a German **widow**, Princess Victoire of Leiningen, with two children, Feodora and Charles. The duke lived abroad, to avoid paying his many debts in England.

None of the older royal princes had sons, so when the duke and duchess learned that a baby was on the way, they delightedly hurried home to England for the birth. On 24 May 1819, baby Victoria was born at Kensington Palace and her father cheerfully declared that she would be queen one day.

◀ A painting by Sir william Beechey of Victoria, aged two, with her mother, the Duchess of Kent.

◄ This portrait of Victoria's father, the Duke of Kent, was painted in 1818. He died before Victoria's first birthday.

Victoria is left alone

Before she was a year old, Victoria lost both her father and grandfather. On 23 January 1820, the Duke of Kent died, having become ill while holidaying in Devon. Then on 29 January, King George III also died. The Prince Regent became King George IV.

Victoria and her mother were left to manage as best they could. In 1821, the London newspapers reported the death of the French Emperor, Napoleon Bonaparte. He had dreamed of ruling Europe. In the new age, what would lie ahead for the little princess?

After Napoleon

In 1815, the Duke of Wellington's army defeated the French Emperor, Napoleon Bonaparte, at the Battle of Waterloo. Europe had been at war almost constantly since the **French Revolution** of 1789. Now there was peace. Governments wanted a return to old ways and old kings, but ordinary people wanted change.

Growing up in a palace

Victoria had a lonely childhood. Her half-brother and sister were grown up and she had no friends of her own age. She lived with her mother in Kensington Palace, a big house in what was then a quiet park in London.

Home life and lessons

The Duchess of Kent was not rich, though she was better off than millions of poor people in Britain. Victoria later wrote that in Kensington Palace 'there was not a single carpet that was not threadbare'. She grew sick of eating **mutton** (the cheapest meat) and a cup of tea was a rare treat.

In 1824, Louise Lehzen came to be Victoria's **governess**. Miss Lehzen was German, clever and strict. After some tantrums, the pupil and teacher became friends and spent happy hours playing with dolls. In 1827, the Reverend George Davys began teaching Victoria Latin, geography, history and religion. The princess spoke fluent German and learned French. She was good at singing and drawing.

▶ Victoria drew this sketch of her governess, Louise Lehzen, in 1833. Victoria described her by saying: 'Though she was most kind, she was very firm.'

Uncle William becomes king

No one was very sad when King George IV died in 1830. Victoria's Uncle William then became king. He and his wife, Queen Adelaide, had two daughters, but both died as babies.

Princess Victoria was kept well away from **court**. Her mother would not even let her go to her Uncle William's **coronation**. Victoria was very disappointed.

In 1830, Miss Lehzen slipped a copy of the royal **family tree** into Victoria's history book. 'I am nearer the throne than I thought', the eleven-year-old cried, and she burst into tears.

▲ This portrait of Victoria was painted by Stephen Smith in 1828, when she was nine years old.

Going to school

Victoria's lessons included learning to walk properly – a sprig of holly tied under her chin made her hold her head up! In the 1830s rich girls were either taught at home like Victoria, or at small private schools. Rich boys had tutors who taught them at home or went away to **boarding schools**. Most poor children had little education.

The roar of progress

In the summers, Victoria lived at Claremont Park, a country house in Surrey. Holidays were spent in Kent at Tunbridge Wells or at the seaside at Ramsgate. Visitors were few. They included her German grandmother Augusta, and her Uncle Leopold. He saw her often until he was asked to become King of the Belgians in 1831.

Hot summers brought outbreaks of disease. Victoria was a healthy child, and survived an attack of dysentery, a stomach bug which caused sickness and diarrhoea and killed many children. She was the first royal child to be **vaccinated** against another killer disease, smallpox.

Changing Britain

Things were changing in industrial Britain. Brilliant scientists and engineers, such as Brunel, Faraday, Stephenson and Babbage, had exciting new ideas. Now iron steamships were crossing the oceans.

Government was still old-fashioned. Even after new laws in 1832, not all men could vote in elections, and women could not vote at all. In 1833 **slavery** was abolished in all British **colonies**, but a year later six farm workers in Dorset were **transported** for trying to form a **trade union**.

▶ This portrait of Victoria, aged seventeen, was painted in 1836 – the year before she became queen.

Travel and a German visitor

Victoria saw the new Britain for herself in 1832, when she was taken on a tour of the Midlands and Wales. In the smoky industrial city of Birmingham, the people looked dirty. She wrote in her diary how shocked she was to see their 'wretched huts and carts and little ragged children'.

In the spring of 1836, when Victoria was 17, her German cousins, Ernest and Albert, came on a visit. She liked them very much, especially Albert who was handsome and 'very clever and intelligent'.

Industrial revolution

By the 1830s, the new factories were changing the landscape of Britain. Tall chimneys belched smoke, factory machines roared and clattered and the red flames from ironworks lit up the night sky. The **industrial revolution** was driven by the power of the steam engine, developed in the 1700s.

▼ Victoria was shocked by the smoky industrial landscapes of the Midlands. The area in this painting by Constantin Meunier was known as the 'Black Country' because of all the factories.

'I am very young...'

On 20 June 1837, Victoria was woken early to be told that her Uncle William was dead. She was now queen, only a month after her eighteenth birthday. 'I am very young', she wrote in her diary, but she promised to 'do her best'. She met Lord Melbourne, the **prime minister**. From now on, she would have to read and sign government papers every day.

Queen in troubled times

Victoria was crowned at Westminster Abbey in London on 28 June 1838. No one knew what to expect, as no woman had reigned since Queen Anne died in 1714.

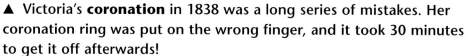

▲ Victoria's **coronation** in 1838 was a long series of mistakes. Her coronation ring was put on the wrong finger, and it took 30 minutes to get it off afterwards!

There were signs of trouble in Britain, and in other countries in Europe. In 1838 soldiers patrolled London's streets, as angry workers marched to demand the same rights as rich people. Through reading Charles Dickens' novel *Oliver Twist*, Victoria learned something of the hard lives of poor people.

Whom to marry?

Victoria liked Lord Melbourne, and turned to him for advice about marriage. The prime minister listed suitable young princes, but Victoria said she would only marry someone she liked. It was agreed to invite her cousin, Albert of Saxe-Coburg, for a second visit.

He arrived in October 1839 and the queen found him, 'beautiful... so amiable and unaffected'. Five days after his arrival at Windsor Castle, Victoria told Albert she wanted to marry him. Albert wrote, 'Heaven has sent me an angel'. Not everyone was happy. A rude verse joked – unfairly – that Albert had come in search of 'England's fat queen and England's fatter purse'.

▲ An illustration by George Cruikshank from *Oliver Twist*. Dickens's story of the horrors of being a poor child shocked the young queen.

Charles Dickens

The writer Charles Dickens was born in 1812. When he was only 12, Dickens worked in a factory, sticking labels on shoe polish bottles. In his late teens he became a newspaper reporter. His best-seller, *Oliver Twist*, was published in 1837, the year Victoria became queen. It told of a London underworld of child criminals and abused **orphans**.

Wedding and revolution

Victoria and Albert were very happy, but Albert soon realized that being the queen's husband would not be easy. He had to stand to one side while Victoria signed new laws or spoke to her ministers. The **prime minister** reminded him that he would always be a prince, never king.

Wedding day

Their wedding took place on 10 February 1840. The queen enjoyed it all – the service in the Chapel Royal at St James's Palace, the crowds, the family congratulations. In November, Victoria gave birth to her first child, a daughter.

In 1840 people in Britain for the first time sent letters with penny stamps, bearing the Queen's head. There was also a new and wonderfully fast means of sending messages – the electric **telegraph**.

▲ This illustration shows the wedding of Victoria and Albert in 1840.

New homes

The queen did not like Buckingham Palace, which was far too gloomy. So the royal couple looked for a more comfortable home of their own. They chose an old house at Osborne, on the Isle of Wight. Prince Albert set about rebuilding the house and grounds of their 'dear little home'.

In 1842 Victoria and Albert visited Scotland. Both fell in love with the Highlands – Albert wore a **kilt**, and the queen wrapped herself in **tartan** scarves. They bought Balmoral Castle in 1847, coming to love it almost as much as Osborne.

Changes

Lord Melbourne resigned in 1841, and Victoria had to get used to new prime ministers: first Robert Peel, then Lord John Russell. She was sad when Melbourne died in 1848.

▲ Sir Francis Grant painted this portrait of Victoria in 1843, three years after she married Albert.

Year of Revolution

1848 was the Year of **Revolution**. In Italy, Germany and Austria people were hungry, out of work and angry at the way they were governed. France's King Louis Philippe was driven out, and a **republic** was set up. There had been famine in Ireland since 1845, because the potato crop was diseased. Many people left Ireland.

The royal family

Many Victorian families were large. Victoria herself had nine children – her first child was born in 1840, her last in 1857.

Bringing up babies

Her first baby was a girl and both Victoria and Albert were 'sadly disappointed' at first. Later the queen became very close to her daughter, Victoria ('Vicky'), who was bright and capable. Victoria's first son, Prince Albert Edward, born in 1841, was known as 'Bertie'. He would be king one day.

Victoria thought that men had little idea of the trouble and pain of childbearing. She was given **chloroform** in 1853 while having her eighth baby, and thought the new pain-relief wonderful.

▲ This 1846 painting of the queen with her family, by the artist Franz Winterhalter, was a favourite of hers.

Braving the bullets

Victoria had several narrow escapes from would-be assassins. In 1840 a 'madman' shot at her, but missed. She was shot at again in 1849, and in 1850 she was hit on the head with a stick. She was cheered at the opera that evening, and wrote in her diary: 'for a man to strike any woman is most brutal'.

In 1842, the queen took her first trip on a steam train, from Slough to Paddington Station in London. She was 'quite charmed' – it was smooth and much safer than riding in an open horse carriage.

Family pleasures

The royal family lived quietly. At Osborne House, Albert laid out a garden for each of their children to work in. There was a model fort, and the children could invite their parents to tea in a small house, called the Swiss Cottage.

▲ The Swiss Cottage at Osborne House on the Isle of Wight, photographed in about 1860. Here Victoria and Albert enjoyed pretending to be an 'ordinary family.

Home life

Most people in Britain lived in small houses or cottages. Rich families had servants to do the housework. Cooks prepared the food. Maids lit coal fires, swept rooms, made beds and washed clothes. At Christmas, families sent cards and lit candles on the Christmas tree – a German custom made popular by Prince Albert.

Workshop of the world

Like many Victorians, Prince Albert believed that education and inventions would bring about a better world of peace and prosperity. So it was no surprise to Victoria when Albert threw his energies into planning the Great Exhibition.

The greatest show on earth

The exhibition was the biggest show of arts, science and industry ever held. The **Crystal Palace** in London's Hyde Park housed 14,000 exhibits from all over the world. It became a showground for the goods produced in Britain's factories. Many people jeered at this 'folly'. They predicted that the building would fall down, thieves would run riot in London and that there would be food shortages and disease.

▲ Items from all over the world were displayed at the Great Exhibition. This painting shows visitors inside the Crystal Palace.

The queen opened the Great Exhibition in May 1851, and throughout the summer she went many times. Six million other visitors came. The exhibition made enough money to pay for new museums and colleges – among them the Natural History Museum, Imperial College and the Victoria and Albert Museum, all of which are still going strong.

Heroes and heroines

In 1852 the Duke of Wellington died. Victoria thought him 'the greatest man this country has ever produced'. How different was her son Bertie, the Prince of Wales. Not good at lessons, and too fond of a good time, Bertie continued to disappoint his parents.

In 1854, Britain went to war in the Crimea. Victoria followed the war news closely and was distressed to read of the sufferings of British troops. She wrote letters of sympathy to **widows** and she and her daughters knitted scarves for the soldiers.

▼ This painting shows Florence Nightingale looking after the sick and wounded in a military hospital in Turkey during the Crimean War.

The Crimean War

This war was fought in the Crimea, a region of Russia edged by the Black Sea. Britain, France and Turkey fought Russia. Many soldiers in the Crimea died from wounds and disease before a group of British nurses, led by Florence Nightingale, set up proper hospitals. The war ended in 1856 without a clear winner.

A queen in mourning

Victoria and Albert were frequent visitors to Europe. In 1855 they were guests of the new French Emperor, Louis Napoleon. He was an attentive host. When told that a table in the queen's apartments was too high for her (she was less than 1.5 metres tall, but hated to think of herself as short), he ordered its legs to be sawn off.

Good times...

The queen was enjoying life thoroughly. In 1858, her daughter Vicky married Prince Frederick, heir to the throne of Prussia, the most important state in Germany. After Vicky left home, the queen missed her very much. She wrote a stream of letters, which became a flood when Vicky had a baby, making Victoria a grandmother at the age of 39.

And the worst time

This happiness did not last. Prince Albert had won most people's admiration for his hard work. When the **American Civil War** began in 1861, the Prince worked even harder to keep Britain out of the war. By the end of the year, he was exhausted.

In December, he became ill. Within two weeks he was dead. Doctors said it was **typhoid fever**. Some blamed the stinking drains at Windsor Castle. No one, rich or poor, was safe from infection in a world without modern drugs.

◀ The queen wore black as she mourned Prince Albert.

The queen was desolate, gripped by 'sickness and icy coldness'. Dressed in **mourning** black, she paid tearful visits to 'dear Albert's room, where all remains the same'. But nothing ever would be the same.

▶ Diseases lurked in smelly drains and dirty water. Many people lived crowded together in city slums. Each public water pump was shared, and there were no proper toilets. This meant diseases, like the typhoid which killed Albert, spread quickly.

The public health

People began to take public health seriously after Dr John Snow, who had given Victoria **chloroform** in childbirth, showed that a **cholera** outbreak in 1854 was caused by people drinking infected water from public pumps. Victorian engineers built water pipes and sewers, many still in use today.

The queen's government

The queen never got over the death of her beloved Albert. She had come to rely on his support, both in her official work and in raising their family. Without him, Victoria felt she could not cope.

Her mother had died in March 1861, not long before Albert. Her favourite government leaders – Melbourne, Peel and Wellington – were dead, too and she did not care for the new men, Palmerston and Gladstone. Only one **prime minister**, Benjamin Disraeli, could charm her with his wit and flattery.

The queen retires

Victoria was only 42 when Albert died, but for almost 40 years she lived more like a retired **widow** than a queen. She said that she was too sad to carry out public duties. She always wore black (the colour of **mourning**) and was seldom seen in public.

The world seen from Scotland

She spent much of her time in Scotland, at Balmoral, receiving messages from London by **telegraph**. She painted and went for pony rides, escorted by her favourite Scottish servant, John Brown. Government ministers came to hate the sight of the blunt-speaking Brown, who seemed to have more influence over the queen than they did.

▶ The queen with her pony, and the faithful John Brown.

Victoria wanted most of all to see her daughters married, and her eldest son Bertie kept out of mischief. She was less interested in international events, though she did fret over the war of 1870 between France and Prussia. France lost, and Victoria felt sorry for the French emperor, but her daughter Vicky was married to a German. Her grandson, Willy, would rule Germany one day.

Freedoms slowly won

The queen was thankful that Britain remained peaceful, especially after France's Emperor Louis Napoleon had to flee Paris during an uprising in 1871. In Britain **reforms** came, but often slowly. In 1871 workers were at last allowed to form **trade unions**, to improve their wages and working conditions.

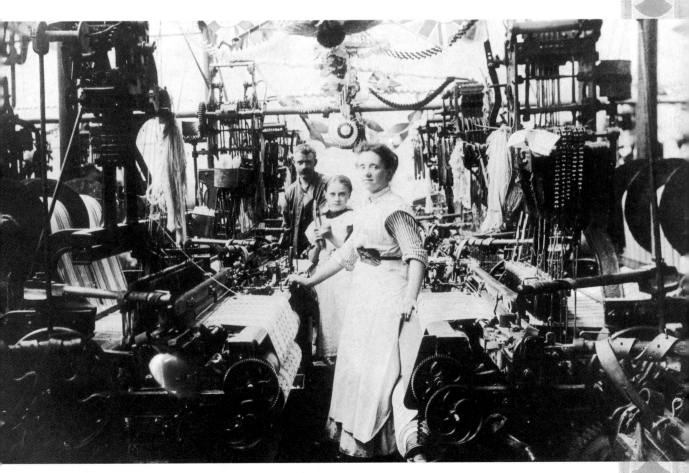

▲ Workers in factories, like this towel mill, worked long hours for low pay. Slowly new laws improved things.

Queen Empress

Victoria never liked **prime minister** William Gladstone, whom she found dull and yet full of dangerous ideas – such as giving **home rule** to Ireland. Worse still, he had little interest in foreign affairs, or the **empire**. She much preferred Benjamin Disraeli, who was 'sound and moderate', and keen to enlarge Britain's empire.

Empress of India

It was Disraeli who suggested in 1876 that she should take a new title, **Empress** of India. India was the largest country within the empire, and Victoria was proud to be empress of some 300 million people.

Keeping in touch

Letters were Victoria's most frequent means of communication. In letters, she told the government what she thought they should do, although they did not always follow her suggestions. She wrote to Vicky about how she enjoyed the operas of Wagner, and how sad she felt at the death of her son Leopold (from **haemophilia**) in 1884. She scolded her German grandson Willy (later Germany's emperor) for being 'impertinent'.

In 1882, Victoria survived a seventh attempt on her life. 'Good, faithful Brown' died in 1883, and his place as favourite servant was taken by the queen's Indian secretary, Abdul Karim. His influence over the queen soon became a new worry to her family and government.

▶ The Queen signing letters, with her Indian secretary, Abdul Karim.

24

Fifty years a queen

The queen was rarely seen in London, except when she opened **Parliament**, but she was more popular than ever. Her Golden Jubilee (50 years as queen) in 1887 was celebrated across the empire with speeches, bands, parades and souvenirs of all kinds.

▲ This painting shows settlers in Sydney, Australia. The Australian states of Queensland and Victoria were named in the Queen's honour.

Imperial queen

Victoria took a keen interest in the empire. She read the news of the African journeys of the explorers Livingstone and Stanley. She learned of settlers from Britain **emigrating** to Canada, South Africa, Australia and New Zealand. Victoria was always eager to hear about India from visitors or her Indian servants.

Jubilee monarch

In 1897 Victoria had been queen for 60 years and celebrated her Diamond Jubilee. By now she was the most famous ruler in the world, and she had relatives in royal families across Europe.

Sixty years on

The celebrations were a triumph and the Queen was 'deeply touched'. Union flags, Jubilee mugs and plates with pictures of the Queen were proudly displayed in houses, big and small.

The guns of Royal Navy battleships boomed salutes, and soldiers of the **empire** in every imaginable uniform lined London's streets for a grand parade. Crowds cheered the queen as she drove in a carriage, wearing a lace bonnet and holding a sunshade. There were so many people pressing to see her that schoolchildren fainted in the hot sun. As part of the Jubilee celebrations, Victoria touched an electric button to send a message by **telegraph** throughout the empire

▲ The elderly queen was driven through cheering crowds to St Paul's Cathedral during the 1897 Diamond Jubilee parade.

The last years

The last war of Victoria's reign began in 1899. The Boer War was fought in South Africa between Dutch-speaking farmers (Boers) and the British army. The queen ordered 100,000 tins of chocolate to be sent to her soldiers. Defeat, she said, was impossible, but the Boers were tough fighters, and for a time things went badly for the British.

The queen was still fit enough to travel to France, but found reading difficult – she complained she could not find 'spectacles to suit'. A century of change was drawing to a close, and the queen's life, too, was nearing its end.

The queen's navy

During Victoria's reign, the British navy was the most powerful in the world. Its ships kept the peace and protected the **trade** routes linking Britain and the empire. In 1894, a new and fast ship, *Turbinia*, showed off its new turbine engines at a naval review.

▲ This painting by Charles Dixon shows ships at the Diamond Jubilee review at Spithead in 1897. Ships of the British navy patrolled the oceans, to defend and enlarge the empire.

After Victoria

Victoria did not live to see the end of the Boer War. In the spring of 1900, she enjoyed a last visit to Ireland, but felt too 'tired and upset' for much more. She lost her appetite and Christmas 1900 at Osborne was miserable. On 23 January 1901, she died, surrounded by her family. Her last words were 'Oh, Albert'.

The queen is dead

Journalists raced away on bicycles with the news. Bertie at last became King Edward VII, at the age of 59. The queen had left strict instructions about her funeral. It was to be white, not black. People who watched the solemn procession never forgot it. Victoria was laid to rest at Frogmore near Windsor, beside Prince Albert. It was a snowy day.

▲ This photograph of Victoria's funeral in 1901 shows the gun carriage carrying her coffin at Green Park, London.

After Victoria

Today Victoria's **empire** is gone, but there are many reminders of the queen. Her name is everywhere on maps: the state of Victoria in Australia, Lake Victoria and the Victoria Falls in Africa, the city of Victoria in British Columbia, Canada, the Victoria mountains in New Zealand. Countless streets and squares are named after her.

Towards the modern world

The Victorian age saw rapid changes in science and industry, and in ordinary life. In many ways, the Victorians created the modern world. They built schools and colleges, tunnels and sewers, public libraries and museums, bridges and railways. Victorian buildings survive in many towns, from terraced houses to town halls. There are **monuments** to Queen Victoria from the Caribbean to Calcutta. Very few people in history have left their mark in so many places.

▲ Statues of Queen Victoria, like this one in Mauritius, show a robed, crowned ruler. Few people saw the ordinary person beneath the crown.

The royal family

Victoria created what we now call the 'royal family'. She made the British **monarchy** more popular, even though its power to make or change laws now belonged to **Parliament**. Queen Elizabeth II is Victoria's great-great-granddaughter, and many more of her descendants are scattered through the royal families of Europe.

Glossary

American Civil War
war fought in 1861–65
between the northern and
southern states of America

boarding schools   schools where
pupils live during term time

chloroform   drug used to ease pain,
by making a person unconscious

cholera   dangerous infectious disease

colony   group of people who move
to live in a new country still ruled
by the country they came from

Commonwealth   association of
countries, most of which were
formerly part of the British Empire

coronation   ceremony of crowning
a new king or queen

court   monarch's palace and the
people who live and work there

Crystal Palace   giant glasshouse
built by Joseph Paxton to house
the 1851 Great Exhibition

emigrating   leaving one country to
make a new life in another

empire   large area of land, ruled over
by a single person

empress   female ruler of an empire

family tree   diagram that shows
how members of a family are
related

French Revolution   violent uprising
in 1789 which removed the
French king and set up a republic

governess   private teacher hired to
teach girls at home

haemophilia   illness causing
frequent bleeding. Haemophilia is
passed on in families. Victoria's
family had the illness.

home rule   government of a region
or country by its own citizens

industrial revolution   changes in
science and industry that began in
Britain in the 1700s, with the
invention of factory machines and
steam engines

kilt   skirt-like garment worn by Scots

monarch   king or queen

monarchy   country ruled by a king
or queen

monument   statue or stone set up in
memory of an important person
or event

mourning   period of sadness after
the death of a loved one. In
Victoria's time, people in
mourning wore black clothes.

mutton   meat from an adult sheep

orphans   children whose parents
have died

Parliament   Britain's law-making
assembly, made up of the House of
Commons and the House of Lords

prime minister   leader of the British
government

reforms   new laws intended to right
wrongs or improve people's lives

regent   person who rules when a
monarch is too young or ill to
govern

republic   a country that is not ruled
by a monarch

revolution   sudden, sometimes
violent, changes in the way things
are done

slavery   forcing people to work
unpaid against their will

tartan   cloth with a checked pattern
worn in Scottish traditional dress

telegraph   electric communications
system invented in the 1830s

trade union   organization formed by
workers to improve their working
conditions and protect their rights

transported   made to live abroad as
a punishment. In Victorian times,
people guilty of certain crimes
could be transported by ship to
Australia and other colonies.

typhoid fever   dangerous disease,
carried by germs in dirty water

vaccinated   given a mild dose of a
disease, to protect against a
dangerous form

widow   woman whose husband has
died

Timeline

1819   Victoria is born in London

1830   King George IV dies, and William IV becomes king.
Britain has world's first passenger-carrying steam railway

1837   William IV dies and Victoria becomes queen

1840   Victoria marries Prince Albert

1842   Doctors first use anaesthetics to ease pain

1851   Queen Victoria and Prince Albert open the Great Exhibition

1854   Britain at war in the Crimea

1861   Prince Albert dies. The American Civil War begins

1865   Joseph Lister pioneers antiseptic surgery

1876   Victoria is named Empress of India.
Alexander Graham Bell demonstrates first telephone

1879   Thomas Edison switches on the first electric light bulb

1887   Victoria's Golden Jubilee is celebrated around the British Empire

1895   X-rays are discovered. Marconi experiments with radio.

1897   Victoria's Diamond Jubilee

1899   The Boer War begins in South Africa

1901   Queen Victoria dies. Edward VII becomes king

Further reading & websites

Groundbreakers series: Charles Darwin, Michael Faraday, Florence Nightingale, Heinemann Library, 2000/2001

Heinemann Explore History: Victorian Britain, Jane Shuter, Heinemann Library, 2001

Life in Victorian Times: Travel and Transport, Neil Morris, Belitha, 1999

Heinemann Explore – an online history resource.
For Key Stage 2 history go to *www.heinemannexplore.com*

www.victorianstation.com/sitemap.htm

www.royal.gov.uk/history/victoria.htm

Places to visit

Osborne House, Isle of Wight   Windsor Castle

Natural History Museum, London   Victoria and Albert Museum, London

Index